MONEY COMING OUT OF MY EARS

Copyright 2017 © by Donna Beserra
All rights reserved
ISBN-13: 978-0-9982826-9-5
Artistic Creations Book Publishing

DEDICATION

This book is dedicated to my dad, who has always been an inspiration to me. He has lived a life of honor and integrity, a great example for his children. My dad has influenced me throughout my life, which has had a great impact on the person I've become. There is no better father than mine. God has blessed me with wonderful parents who have lovingly motivated me to develop my talents.

DONNA BESERRA

MONEY COMING OUT OF MY EARS

by: Donna Beserra

Starring in Our Own Movies

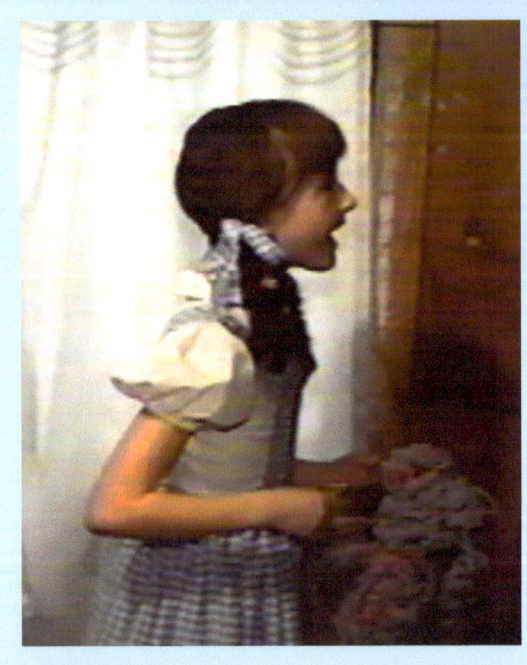

(Photos captured from homemade video)

A New Family Fairy Tale

Several years ago someone asked me if I thought I would ever make any money on the children's books I was publishing. My semi-serious reply was, "I'll have money coming out of my ears." At the time I didn't realize the significance of that statement, and I know you are probably wondering whether or not I am making a lot of money. By the time this book is finished, we should have an answer to that question.

Of course, money was not my original motivation for writing books. It had all begun because of a hobby I shared with my children. When my kids (Nadia, Sabrina, Donnie and Shereene) were very young, they loved acting out their favorite fairy tales. In order to encourage their creativity, I began making costumes and allowing them to perform the stories on home video. My grandson Trent later became part of our cast. We truly enjoyed making our movies.

Eventually, I decided to create a fairy tale of my own. I invented a character called Twirly Shirley, a little girl whose braided hair twirled when she became emotional. I made a set of spinning braids and we performed our story, *Twirly Shirley in My Sister the Twister,* on home video. We even created a photo book of our fairy tale. It turned out so well, I decided to publish the book so we could share it with others. I sent in a copy of my book and video to the copyright office to protect my work.

My first publishing experience was with a print-on-demand company. With the help of my oldest daughter Nadia, I submitted the book and the fee to them. The kids and I were very excited when we got our first copy in the mail. We thought for sure the book would be a best-seller. That wasn't exactly what happened, yet it was a wonderful experience just having a book published.

I informed the media about our book, and we were called in for a news interview. The station wasn't only interested in the book itself. They were even more interested in how it came to be. They wanted us to explain how our family hobby had evolved into published work. Sabrina, Donnie and Shereene participated in the interview, each of them adding their own input about our publishing adventure. Donnie even talked about the "technical difficulties" we had encountered filming our movie.

I had ideas for new Twirly Shirley stories, but I felt my original approach to publishing was too costly. I heard about a class on self-publishing being offered at a community college. It was being taught by Barbara McPherson, a successful published author. I decided I would take the class. I learned all about designing a book layout, as well as how to obtain an ISBN and LCCN. There were many other steps included in the process, which I will go over later. There was a lot of work to be done, but I did it all.

Inventions and Fairy Tales

Gazette Photo by Mark Christian

"Sometimes wackiness is Mother of Invention"

This was the headline published in the Cedar Rapids Gazette. My son Donnie and I are pictured in the above photo. The article goes on to describe how Donnie "repairs a loose wire on his "Wacky Spinmobile" while his mother, Donna watches last night during the Science and Hobby Fair at Johnson School of the Arts in Cedar Rapids Thursday March 14, 2002."

This was a special time for my kids and I. We had been making our own movies for years, when Donnie became interested in inventions. I purchased a book for him, so he could learn to create his own gadgets. I helped him build a little car for entry in his school science fair. Instead of running in the usual straight line however, the car spun in circles. Donnie added a red blinking light which made it look like a miniature spaceship. Donnie named his invention the Wacky Spinmobile, which described it perfectly.

We had been really getting into making things spin. I made an Inspector Gadget Costume for Donnie, complete with a spinning helicopter hat. Eventually, I designed a set of spinning braids for Twirly Shirley. My daughter Shereene wore the braids and starred in our movie, *Twirly Shirley in My Sister the Twister*. The other children played parts in the movie as well. So I suppose wackiness really can be Mother of Invention!

I worked like mad to complete my Christmas Book, *Twirly Shirley and the Brother Like No Other* in time for the holiday season. I published it early enough, and submitted information to local news stations. I was hoping to get an interview prior to Christmas. I ended up getting one in the middle of January, which I thought was a little too late.

Our interview was scheduled for a school day, and my children were disappointed about missing classes. It turned out school was canceled due to bad weather. It worked out great for us because the roads were clear, and teachers were home watching the news! We were invited to schools to inspire kids to read and write.

I published my third Twirly Shirley book, *Twirly Shirley in Hurricane Shirley*. I illustrated it using photos of the children as I had done with the other books, only this time I added some computer art. I was not an artist, but I did the best I could.

I had struggled with having books printed because of the high cost. I decided to print the books myself this time, but I had to have them spiral bound. My books did look homemade, which wasn't necessarily a bad thing. The printer was using too much ink however, and that was a problem.

Did either of these books make the best-seller list? Not quite. I did continue to visit schools to give speeches to motivate children to read and write. Once a little boy asked me if I was a millionaire. The teacher explained that people don't only write books for the money. She was right about that, but just between us, I think I would have enjoyed being a millionaire. Who wouldn't?

As I continued publishing books, it became even more expensive. I didn't give up though. I know that I would have published my stories no matter what, even if I knew that I would never make a profit. It was something I was meant to do, and God always provided a way for me to get help with the cost.

My books and school visits entertained, educated and inspired children. I felt good about that. One little girl announced that since hearing about Twirly Shirley she had developed an interest in writing she'd never had before. Her mother was especially excited about her new found interest.

During the time I was busy publishing Twirly Shirley books, I was approached by Barbara McPherson about a project she was working on. It was a book about missing shoes, and Barb was gathering local authors together to write stories about how the shoes disappeared. I thought it was a great opportunity, so I signed up. My children, Sabrina (age 14), Donnie (age 13), and Shereene (age 9) wrote stories as well. The book was titled *Lost Soles* and was written by a collection of about 18 authors. The editors had made some unexpected changes to my story, but that often happens when a book is published by someone other than the author. There was some talk of *Lost Soles* becoming a movie or television series. Either one probably would have been successful. The book did include some interesting stories.

I was called in to do a news interview for *Lost Soles.* At the interview I was also given an opportunity to introduce Twirly Shirley to a new audience. I discussed how Twirly Shirley teaches children about dealing with their emotions, and I announced two upcoming book signings at local book stores.

During one of my book signings, I met a wonderful fellow author. I talked with her about the Twirly Shirley books, and she suggested I contact her publisher about the stories. She felt he might be interested in publishing the Twirly Shirley Series.

Until now I had not contacted many publishers about my work, because I had already heard about how difficult and time-consuming it could be just to find one who would read the manuscript. That isn't even including the time and effort the publishing process would take if the material was accepted. I had pretty much settled on doing it myself, but I decided to give someone else a try just this once. I got a copy of the book together, along with some other materials, and a copy of the video. I sent them in and awaited a reply.

Barbara McPherson had helped me immensely. I had asked her if she was planning to teach another class. She replied, "Next time you teach it." I was a little stunned, because I certainly did not feel qualified. I decided to give it a shot anyway because I needed a job. I also knew that God would be with me. I applied and was hired to teach at Black Hawk College Outreach Center.

I worked hard to prepare the lessons for my self-publishing class. I was very nervous, because I had never taught this subject before. My class consisted of a variety of students including a teacher, an artist and even a Baptist minister. I felt a little intimidated at first, but realized I did know what I was doing. After all, I had published three times already.

I was pleasantly surprised to learn that the artist, Melody Karns Trone, was a someone I had met as a child. We attended the same church and became friends when we were both teenagers. We had not seen each other in over twenty years. I was thrilled to see her again. She was a very special person. In fact, she had prayed with me the day I accepted Jesus as my Lord and Savior. At the time I was only 14 years old.

Melody had created a beautiful book of her own. She decided to help me by painting an illustration for *Twirly Shirley in My Sister the Twister* to be sent to the publisher. I sent copies of the Twirly Shirley books in as well, and although he stated he was impressed, the publisher said he didn't have the right market for them. He suggested that I self-publish new versions. The publisher explained that many of his customers were farmers, and he requested that I write books about farm animals to submit to him.

Meanwhile, Melody and I decided to go ahead and create a new version of *Twirly Shirley in My Sister the Twister* illustrated by Melody. The characters would be based on my children as in the original book. As I said before, I was not an artist, so Melody rescued my book with her wonderful illustrations.

I had to purchase a new computer in order to set up my book layout, and once again I ran into production difficulties. Having books printed by a professional printer was extremely costly. The price per book went down somewhat as the quantity increased, however I only needed a small number of books to start out.

I tried various methods of getting the books printed, but none of them worked out very well. The prices were high and the quality of the printing was not up to my expectations. I decided once again to do the job myself. I purchased a large format ink-jet printer, but found the ink ran out very quickly and I just couldn't keep up. I finally decided to rent-to-own a high quality laser printer. I was using the saddle stitch method (stapled spine) because I had no other binding equipment available.

I later published new versions of *Twirly Shirley in Hurricane Shirley* and *Twirly Shirley and the Brother Like No Other.* Once again Melody came to the rescue with her beautiful artwork. While Melody was still working on illustrations for *Twirly Shirley and the Brother Like No Other,* an article about my new business was printed in the Moline Dispatch-Rock Island Argus newspaper (by Nick Loomis and staff).

The article explained how my business had started. It also mentioned that I had taken publishing and business classes to prepare myself to become a publisher. When questioned about the biggest hurdle I had overcome, I replied, "It's a toss-up between financial difficulty, and the problems associated in dealing with computers. Computer work can be complicated. Being able to produce books at a reasonable cost can also be difficult."

The new versions of Twirly Shirley were somewhat popular, but still didn't exactly get on the best-seller list. In fact, I was still not making a profit. I did manage to get them in Barnes & Noble and Borders Book Stores. It was difficult since I was required to have the books listed with Partners Book Distributors. I had to go through a lot of red tape, but managed to get in. I had some author signing events with the book stores.

New Business Profile

Nick Loomis/staff

Above is a photo that was published in the Moline Dispatch-Rock Island Argus in Moline, Illinois in September of 2007. I had just recently begun publishing new versions of my books which were being illustrated by Melody Karns Trone. The article included important information about my business and how it was started.

I was given an opportunity to discuss some of the hurdles I had overcome including financial difficulties, complications with computers and the problem of "being able to produce books at a reasonable cost".

Twirly Shirley Takes Off!

Sirens sound! People scramble for cover! The whole town is in a panic as a tornado rages overhead! Twirly Shirley is twisting the town inside out. Shirley has a tendency to get "wound up", and when she does it creates pure chaos. The question is, how does she do it? What is the secret behind Shirley's super spectacular abilities?

Pictured here is the latest version of my very first story, Twirly Shirley in My Sister the Twister. Artist Melody Karns Trone has based some of her illustrations on my children, who were the stars in the original series of books and videos.

The Twirly Shirley character helps children learn to deal with their emotions. When Shirley's emotions get out of control, her braids begin spinning wildly. This causes all kinds of catastrophes to occur. When Shirley calms down, her braids cease to spin and things are peaceful once again.

Hurricane Shirley is Coming!

Look out everyone! Hurricane Shirley is surging across the ocean. People frantically seek refuge as sea creatures dive to the bottom of the water, but don't worry. This isn't your typical hurricane. It's just Twirly Shirley, the girl with the incredible spinning braids. She's twirled up another cyclone, only this one is on the open sea. Be sure to join Shirley for a great tropical adventure. You'll be glad you did!

Pictured above is the latest version of Twirly Shirley in Hurricane Shirley. Melody has once again based the characters on my children. Other illustrations can be seen below.

Original Hurricane Shirley

The original characters from the Twirly Shirley Series are pictured in the above photos. The photo on the right is of my son Donnie and grandson Trent, who starred as news reporters in Twirly Shirley in Hurricane Shirley. Sabrina is narrator in most of the books. Nadia played various roles, and helped with photography and videography. Donnie and Trent had additional parts in Twirly Shirley and the Brother like no other.

My children are all very creative, and they have been a great inspiration to me. Some of their interests influenced material in my books.

New Christmas Edition

The wind is howling and snow is swirling. Knees are knocking and teeth are chattering. Everyone in the room has frosted hair. Is this the North Pole? Not exactly. It's just the school Christmas Program starring the girl with the famous spinning braids. Twirly Shirley has created a snow storm right in the middle of the school auditorium.

Twirly Shirley and the Brother Like No Other combines the adventures of Twirly Shirley with a lesson about love and forgiveness. This story will entertain young and old alike. Does anyone out there have a brother like no other? If you do, be sure to read this book.

So join in with the audience for a spectacular performance. Just be sure to dress warm and sit a few rows back. You never know when Shirley might get wound up again, and you could find yourself in the middle of a blizzard!

Above is a picture and a blurb from my newest version of *Twirly Shirley and the Brother Like No Other*.

More Publishing Details

I would like to get a little bit deeper into my procedures for publishing books, although I won't include all of them, (because they are numerous, and some methods of publishing have changed in recent years). I'd like to begin with the fact that I consulted my local SCORE (an organization that offers free assistance to entrepreneurs). SCORE provides mentoring from expert volunteers, who not only offer guidance, but also assist with other resources for businesses.

Another important beginning step for me was to obtain ISBNs (International Standard Book Numbers) Each book title must have a unique number which identifies it. I visited Bowker's website where I filled out a form, and purchased a set of 10 ISBNs. This is also how I became the publisher. I printed the appropriate number inside each book.

Next I ordered a barcode for each title, which I placed on the back cover. The barcode included the ISBN and the price I had decided on. The barcode was also purchased from Bowker. Once I had published the book I registered it with Bowker Books in Print. This would allow the book to be discovered.

After I had registered the title I visited the Library of Congress website in order to obtain an LCCN (Library of Congress Control Number). I filled out the information and mailed a copy of the book to them.

Of course I wanted my books to be available in book stores. Many of the stores purchased books through a distributor. I applied through Partners Book Distributors. I had to go through quite a few hassles, but my books were accepted and Partners ordered some copies, which I printed and mailed to them.

Once I had the books available, I wrote news releases, which I then emailed to newspapers and television stations. Some samples can be seen next to the pictures of the books on the preceding pages. I also made phone calls. This is how I obtained some of my interviews and was able to have articles printed about my books.

Besides advertising through news media, I also looked for local events where I could promote my books. I continued to visit schools and children's organizations. I printed flyers and business cards, which I distributed wherever I could.

Another step I took to help advance my books was to request reviews from people who had read the stories. Good reviews can really help with the promotion of a book. The reviews of my books helped get them accepted by Partners Book Distributors, and also got them noticed by the media and book stores.

Creative Creatures Interactive Books

Now I'd like to get back to those farm creature books. The publisher I contacted had requested a book about a worm in an apple. It was to be told from a worm's point of view. I got to work and finished the story. I sent in an apple shaped book with a small puppet. To my disappointment, the publisher decided that it might not be a good idea to use a worm in the book. I rewrote the story using a butterfly instead. The book was titled *Buffy the Butterfly's Apple Orchard*. While he reviewed this book, the publisher requested that I write more farm creature stories. I wrote a book titled *Barton the Bat's Pumpkin Patch*.

Writing these stories reminded me of my childhood, at which time I had written from a cat's point of view. Here I was once again writing in the same style I had used when I was very young. I created a pumpkin shaped book which I mailed in to the publisher. I patiently awaited a response.

My next story was *Maurice the Mouse's Cornfield*, which reminded me of a very intriguing dream I had in my early publishing days. To summarize, I had traveled away from my home. I was sitting at a table in what seemed to be in a small restaurant. People were gathering around me and treating me like a celebrity. They were piling money on the table, as if to make some type of purchase. I was puzzled by what was happening.

On the way home from the restaurant, I got lost. All I could see ahead of me on both sides of the road were endless rows of corn. My heart was racing. I began to drive faster and faster. I thought to myself, "Here I am going so fast, and I don't even know if I'm going the right way!" The dream baffled me, but I felt it had meaning. I looked up cornfields in a book on dreams. Cornfields were said to represent prosperity. I also recollected my comment about having "money coming out of my ears". Could there be a connection? I wondered.

While writing these farm books, I began to notice a pattern. They were interactive and encouraged kids to discover their talents. I knew these ideas were developing into a series. I searched my mind for a name to describe the series. I came up with Creative Creatures. Then a slogan came to me:

Creative Creatures

**Creative Creatures help parents and teachers
achieve their goals to educate by helping children to create.
Now kids look deep inside themselves and leave their gadgets on the shelves.
Creative Creatures make learning fun, and this adventure has just begun.
There are more creatures on the way. Creative Creatures are here to stay....
so get those little brains a'tickin with new ideas that keep on clickin'.**

This was all a surprise to me. It wasn't what I had planned. I loved the concept however. I had always encouraged my own kids to discover and develop their talents, and now I would be able to inspire other children as well. I truly believed this concept was God sent. I submitted the rest of the materials to the publisher.

He said he really liked the Creative Creatures idea, but I did not hear back from him about publishing the stories. I decided to self-publish them. Melody created the illustrations for *Buffy the Butterfly's Apple Orchard* and *Barton the Bat's Pumpkin Patch*. They were very creative illustrations and cleverly done.

During these early publishing days I had continued to work with kids, visiting schools and children's organizations. I even directed performances of my Twirly Shirley stories throughout the community. They were very popular.

As you probably noticed from the Creative Creatures slogan, my original plan was to get the books into the hands of parents and teachers so they could use the stories to inspire children. Well, guess what. I had become the teacher.

As I was publishing the Creative Creatures I began a new project based on my stories. I produced my very own television show called *Discover Your Talent*. The first show was about *Buffy the Butterfly's Apple Orchard*. I read the story, and filmed my visit to a real apple orchard.

The next show was about *Barton the Bat's Pumpkin Patch*. Of course I visited pumpkin patches and gathered more information to teach kids. I read my story and even included some funny video clips to entertain the viewers. I also produced shows based on the Twirly Shirley Books.

Besides *Maurice the Mouse's Cornfield,* I added *Pirate the Parrot's Tropical Treasure,* and *Sabrina Ballerina and Kitty Catarina* to the Creative Creatures Series. I also added another book to the Twirly Shirley Collection. This book was called *Twirly Shirley and the Tsunami Mommy*. I ended up illustrating these other books myself. As I've mentioned, I was not an artist, but my goal was to get them published.

Eventually I got an opportunity to teach a class at Black Hawk College based on *Maurice the Mouse's Cornfield.* It was a corn detasseling adventure told from a mouse's perspective, and was designed to inspire kids to become storytellers and writers. I taught the kids to write and illustrate their own books. I was impressed with how hard the children worked. Parents were invited as the kids shared their stories. We had a small reception afterward. I had created a *Maurice the Mouse's Candy Cornfield Cake* topped with gummy mice for the students and guests.

I produced a *Discover Your Talent Show* based on *Maurice the Mouse's Cornfield*. Since the story was told from a mouse's point of view, I included spooky background music as the detasselers (giants) trampled Maurice's cornfield.

I ended up teaching more classes. I taught a *Movie Making* Class based on *Buffy the Butterfly's Apple Orchard*. I brought in scene setters and supplies. The students were involved in various aspects of making a movie. Each child had an acting part. They were also allowed to help with the photography and planning. The students created posters and flyers inviting their families to a movie premier. I produced the movie.

On the last day the students made popcorn, and helped with refreshments for the families who came to watch our movie on the big screen. The children were called by name to come up and receive awards after the show. The class was a great success, and the kids were very proud of our movie.

The following week I taught a *Discover Your Talent* Class based on *Pirate the Parrot's Tropical Treasure*. We created a movie from this story as well. I brought in costumes and props as I had done with the other class. I was pleased to see shy children building confidence and getting involved in the movie-making process. Besides a movie, we also added a talent show allowing the students to showcase their special skills. This was shown to the families on the big screen, and these students received awards of their own.

After I finished teaching the classes at Black Hawk, I began working in local schools as a paraeducator. I would travel from one school to another, and had many opportunities to share my stories with students of various ages. The Twirly Shirley books were a hit. Children loved them, and would often begin writing their own stories after listening to mine.

I took on a second job while working at the schools. I became a portrait photographer. I had always loved photography, so I was happy to get paid to take pictures. I had been using an Adobe photo program to illustrate my books, and was able to use similar tools to create photo collages for customers. The job turned out to be temporary, but I was ready to move on to other projects.

After awhile I was offered a position as a reading instructor at one of the schools I had been working at. I had quite a bit of experience teaching reading and I was glad to accept the position. I worked one on one with students. This job led into another position of documentary filmmaking instructor for middle school kids.

The funding for my job with the school soon ran out. My books stopped selling as well. In fact, Partners Book Distributors began returning books and eventually dropped me because of lack of orders. To top it all off, I had to endure criticism from people who were downgrading my books. These people were saying my books were unsuccessful because they were not selling well, therefore not making money.

The critisism upset me, so I spoke Pastor Chuck Kurth. He prayed with me for increased book sales, but he also reminded me that if just one child had been blessed by a book I had published, it was all worthwhile. I realized he was absolutely right. I also realized I had allowed myself to be defined by society's idea of success, which often times revolves around the amount of money an individual is making. I decided not to allow myself to be brought down by the negativity of critical people.

There is nothing wrong with making money on something worthwhile, but that is not all it is about. It is possible for a person to be successful even without being wealthy. In reality I was already a very successful person. My dream of becoming an author had been fulfilled, and I knew at least a few children who had been blessed by my books. I had many reasons to be thankful.

Yet even though I was aware of all this, I still hoped to someday acquire financial prosperity. After all, I had invested so much time and effort into these books. Not to mention the expense that I had not yet recovered. This was, in fact a business, and a business is supposed to make a profit. Not only had I not made a profit. I wasn't even close to breaking even. I believed it was God's will for his people to prosper in every way, so I was expecting to begin selling more books.

At the same time this all was happening, I had been having printer problems which were very expensive to repair. It had happened just as I had gotten the rent-to-own printer paid off. This was very frustrating for me, but since the books had practically stopped selling I didn't really need to print many copies anyway. I just put the repairs on hold and moved on.

I was still hoping business would pick up, but I kind of went on with life. Then one day while I was attending a church service, a gentleman approached to tell me not to worry about my books. "It's God's mission. He opens the doors" he declared. That statement really made me think. I believed there was a divine purpose for what I was doing. It had already occurred to me while the Creative Creatures stories were developing. I had felt as if they were being written through me instead of by me.

The unique children and creatures in each of the books emphasize the fact that every child is special with his or her own set of talents. For example, *Buffy the Butterfly's Apple Orchard* features Jessica (a singer), and Buffy the Butterfly (a dancer). Buffy not only promotes healthy eating, she also invites kids to join in the adventure; "Just put down that candy bar. Grab an apple and be a star!"

I had always believed that God has given each of us talent that we are to develop. I felt that God was getting the message across through me and my Creative Creatures

Book Series. I still believed that God had a plan for me, and a purpose for my books. Yet everything seemed to be at a standstill. That is why I put the books "on the shelf" for the time being.

Taking Another Path

I was disappointed, but thought maybe I should go down a different path. Pastor Kurth had preached a message about "being in God's waiting room". Maybe that's where I was as far as my books were concerned. Anyhow, my real dream was to produce movies. I decided to get some training. I searched for animation programs, but found none in my area. I decided I would go to Black Hawk College to obtain an Art Technology Certificate. After all, illustrating was part of animation. I studied computer programming and flash programming as well.

I began working as a production assistant at WQAD Channel 8 news. I operated the cameras and teleprompter during newscasts, cooking and sports shows, telethons and an even a political debate. I eventually began editing and producing episodics.

The production assistant position worked well with my classes. It was part time, so I was still able to go to school and study. I did end up working almost constantly however. When I wasn't at work with WQAD, I was at school or busy studying or doing homework. I was determined to do my very best, so I kept my grades high and learned as much as I could.

As I was going on with my life, I came across Walmart's Get on the Shelf Contest. I decided to submit my books. Shortly afterward I received word that my Twirly Shirley Series was chosen for entry in the contest! I thought this could be the break I was waiting for, but it was up to me to get as many votes for my product as possible.

I immediately went to work contacting everyone I could think of to ask for their votes. I called and emailed friends. I used social media to ask for votes as well. I even had a TV news interview to help advertise. It was difficult, because not only did I have to get people to vote, I needed to get them to vote every single day through the end of the contest. In order to win I had to acquire the most votes, and I was up against other people and their products across the country. Unfortunately I did not win the contest, so I put the books back on the shelf once again.

I continued on with my studies at Black Hawk. I would work on art projects and study during my breaks at Channel 8. One of my requirements for graduation from Black Hawk College was that I would complete a class in digital photography. I still had a great interest in photography and video. I had created photo and video biographies for my children. I included scenes throughout their lives. I had managed to get a video of Donnie before he was born. I was able to create a DVD of his life, ultrasound through graduation. On Sabrina's 22nd birthday I showed a DVD with clips from all her birthdays up until that point. I did the same for my other children as well. It was amazing to see them change right before our eyes.

I graduated from Black Hawk College in December of 2013. I had received a student's discount to download Adobe Creative Cloud onto my computer. I had begun working on an animated version of *Twirly Shirley in My Sister the Twister*. I had no training with Adobe movie programs so I had to learn them on my own.

Before long a new teaching opportunity came my way. I became a Black Hawk College for Kids Instructor teaching Photoshop Elements. I had worked many years with Photoshop, so this was a good fit for me. It was very rewarding watching the students as they were learning, developing their own ideas and creating their own projects, which were pretty awesome. College for Kids only lasted one week, but I was invited to return the next year and I have been back every year since.

I quickly got back to my movie-making project. The process of animating my movie was going very slowly. I spent nearly three months working on a particularly complicated clip that was only one and a half seconds in duration. Fortunately most of the other clips were a little less complicated, but animating was very time-consuming. I began to wonder when I would ever finish.

Soon I began working as a paraeducator again. I had opportunities to share my books with the students from several schools. I was even able to help students in one of the classes with stories of their own. The children were becoming very interested in my books again. Interest began growing among the teachers and librarians as well. They were asking how they could order books. Unfortunately not many of them were available any more. I had almost given up on the books, but now my interest was being reignited.

My new problem was being able to create more books and make them available once again. So many doors had been slammed shut on me. I had no printer, no distributor, and no place to sell the books. I prayed for a solution, and shortly thereafter I found one.

I had been shopping for a new printer. I felt it would be less expensive than repairing my Okidata. I stopped into a store to look around. A young salesman was showing me some of their models. He asked me what I was planning to use the printer for. When I explained that I was publishing books he told me that an ordinary printer would wear out very quickly. He suggested that I contact Createspace, a company owned by Amazon. He said he had published a book with them, and he was very pleased with their work. Best of all it was free! It sounded almost too good to be true, but I went home and quickly looked them up.

It wasn't long before I was preparing my first book, *Twirly Shirley in My Sister the Twister* for publication through Createspace. Through my education with Black Hawk College I had learned to work with Adobe InDesign. It was excellent for creating a book layout. All the text and illustrations went easily into the document. I already had the illustrations Melody had created. I just needed to rescan the originals.

Createspace has a few options for publishing through them. They offer a free ISBN. This is one of their own. It is good because it allows the author to make his or her book available through each of Createspace's different channels. The author is restricted from printing the book containing their ISBN with other sources though.

Since I already owned an unused ISBN through my own publishing company, I decided to use that for my new book version. I would still be able to sell my book through Createspace channels with a few exceptions. I did decide to publish another version using a Createspace ISBN however.

I chose a font for the title of my book, and then picked one for the body. My story was written in rhyme so I needed a font that fit the pages well and was easy to read. I then placed the illustrations on alternating pages. I also included a copyright and dedication. I divided my book into 32 pages which is standard for a children's picture book.

I realize some of this information might be confusing to a new author, but Createspace provides a lot of helpful information on their website, including articles on creating and instructions on formatting. They even supply a cover creator to help the author design a professional looking book cover.

Once my book was completed to my satisfaction, I converted it to a PDF file as was required. I had included a bleed in my document which meant the pictures would cover the entire page with no white edges. I checked "use document settings" for the bleed to be included in the PDF.

I must mention that it took quite a few tries to get my document ready to be converted. Although I completed spell checks in case of typos, and looked the document over repeatedly I kept finding adjustments that needed to be made. Even after creating the PDF file, I still discovered more changes that were necessary.

Eventually I was satisfied enough to submit my interior file to Createspace. They have a very helpful interior reviewer that searches the document for errors before Createspace will accept it for review by their team. Createspace will notify the author if changes need to be made. The author can make corrections and submit the document as many times as necessary.

I used Createspace's Cover Creator to design my book's exterior. I created both front and back using Photoshop and InDesign. With Cover Creator I chose a layout design, then inserted my front and back cover. I chose a color for the book's spine and uploaded the file to Createspace. From there I could view it up close to decide whether I approved of it.

Once I had approved of my interior and exterior files, I uploaded them to Createspace for review by their team. This is a process that can take up to 24 hours. Createspace will then determine if the files meet their standards for being printed. If the files don't meet Createspace's requirements, the author must make changes and resubmit files. If Createspace determines the files are printable, the author can review them Online and/or order a printed proof. From there the author can decide to move forward with publishing or to revise the work and resubmit.

Although I was satisfied with my digital files, I ordered a proof just to be sure the printed version of the book was what I was hoping for. I was extremely pleased with the results. The printed proof looked beautiful and very professional. The colors were vibrant, and the book was very well designed with perfect binding. (No more saddle stitch).

I quickly began advertising and set up a book signing event with Barnes & Noble. The new books went over very well and the Barnes & Noble store sold out. I quickly began working on my next book, *Twirly Shirley in Hurricane Shirley*. I completed the publishing and set up another author signing event at Barnes & Noble.

I published *Buffy the Butterfly's Apple Orchard* and *Barton the Bat's Pumpkin Patch* for the Fall. The original books were smaller, and Melody had illustrated them on a white background. I decided to change to a sky blue background. It looked great.

I did find one complication with publishing through Createspace. I was having difficulty having books placed in Barnes & Noble. Although they would sometimes purchase them in limited quantities, many of the stores were reluctant to deal with Createspace because of their no return policy. I had to find another option for getting them into the book stores.

I decided to publish with Ingram Spark. I would need to purchase new ISBNs, and pay fees, but I felt it was necessary to have books placed in the stores. I started with *Twirly Shirley in My Sister the Twister*. I was fortunate because I had already published with my own ISBN through Createspace. I just needed to have the files transferred over to Ingram. It was wonderful because I didn't need to design a book layout or make any changes. Ingram just took over distribution of the title.

I continued publishing with Createspace because I really liked their work and helpfulness. I published *Twirly Shirley and the Brother Like No Other*. I created a special candy cane design for the cover font. Createspace did an excellent job with this book also. Unfortunately I was unable to have a book signing for this title.

I published *Twirly Shirley and the Brother Like No Other* with Ingram Spark as well. It was more complicated this time. I had to purchase an ISBN. I had to redesign the book and cover. Ingram had different specifications than Createspace did.

I decided to publish a whole new book in time for Christmas. I had written a story a few years before called *Christmas in Heaven*. I had a lot of work ahead of me because I would have to design a layout from scratch, and I would need to illustrate the book myself. I worked diligently for long hours preparing the book for publication. My art skills had greatly improved since I had studied at Black Hawk, but now they were really being put to the test. I finished my book and put it through the publishing process with Createspace and Ingram.

Because I intended to continue publishing with Ingram Spark, I had purchased a set of 10 ISBNs from Bowker. I now had two Christmas books ready for the holiday season. I decided to publish *Christmas in Heaven* on Kindle. I had not done this with any of the other books, but since this was a special Christian story, I wanted it to be available in additional formats. I also published a digital version of the book with Ingram. Each version required a separate ISBN.

I didn't have any book store events in time for Christmas. However, I did advertise and promote books on Small Business Saturday. I was able to post photos, and I created special pages for each book on social media. The books were getting noticed. There were a lot of viewings and likes.

Christmas came and went. Since I was headed to Texas in January to visit family, I decided it would be a good idea to promote my books while I was there. I had a book signing at a Barnes & Noble store in Dallas. It was very nice. I also had one at a Barnes & Noble in McCallen Texas. I really enjoyed it because I was able to read one of the books to groups of children. They seemed very entertained and asked lots of questions. The books were well liked in Texas.

I did make some small royalties from sales to Barnes & Noble. Because of production costs and the bookstore discounts, I made very little per book, yet at least it was something. I didn't receive any royalties from digital books however.

I had already started working on my next book, a new version of *Twirly Shirley and the Tsunami Mommy*. I got right back at it when I returned from Texas. The artwork

I was creating was very difficult for me. I had decided I would promote this book for Mother's Day. I was drawing illustrations of my family members. I wanted the first book to go to my mother, Shirley. I included both my parents, myself, my children, all my grandchildren and even one of my brothers as characters in the book.

I struggled a great deal with illustrating this book. In addition to making the characters resemble my relatives, I also had to create pictures of a tsunami, ocean scenes and sea creatures. I didn't have experience with a lot of this. I prayed, asking God to guide me. He heard my prayer and enabled me to create illustrations I was happy with. I published the book with Createspace and Ingram.

I discovered that my local Barnes & Noble store was not having any more author events. I was discouraged once again, but I did have another chance to promote my books. My church, MGT New Hope, hosted an event called Azusa Midwest. I was able to attend services. I also had a booth set up to sell books during the breaks.

A young man came by my table during one of the intermissions. He asked me if he could pray for me. I can't recall all his prayer, but the young man did mention that God had seen me struggling with my artwork. He went on to say that God was going to help me by making it easier for me. He also said that God was going to multiply. He repeated three times "He's going to multiply it and multiply it and multiply it!"

After the break I went in to the service. We sang and worshiped God. Then people gathered at the front to be prayed for. I went up as well. As I was standing there praying, one of the guest speakers walked up to me. She declared, "You've been waiting for something for a very long time. The Lord just showed me it's right around the corner, it's right around the corner, it's right around the corner." She placed her hand on forehead and I fell to the floor. Once again I'd had a word from God repeated to me three times. I knew now that my breakthrough was very close.

Although I had sold a few books during Azusa, the sales seemed to come to a halt Online. Most frequently I saw a big zero next to my royalties. It was really hard for me to believe that no books were selling. That almost seemed impossible. I thought somebody, somewhere had to be buying books.

Prayers had gone out for success with the book sales. I had often prayed with my church friends. One of the ladies who prayed with me declared that it would happen in a way I did not expect. I remembered the words that had been spoken over the books throughout the years, and I held on to those words. I knew that an increase of success and prosperity for my books was "right around the corner". I held on tightly to my faith, in spite of the way things looked. I knew God had something really special in store, beyond what I could even imagine.

Christmas in Heaven

"This book is dedicated to those whose loved ones have left this world to be in Heaven with Jesus.

"It was two weeks before Christmas and six-year-old Julie was full of anticipation. Her parents, Dave and Carol had taught little Julie about the true meaning of Christmas. Carol would always read the bible story of Christ's birth. Then the family would pray and sing happy birthday to Jesus before opening their gifts."

This year Carol had become very ill. Little Julie found a very special Christmas gift for her mother. The little girl thought this gift would help her mom feel better, but what would happen if Carol didn't survive through the holiday season?

Above is a photo and quote from my new book, Christmas in Heaven. I decided to make this book available in digital format as well as in paperback. It is available on Amazon Kindle and Barnes & Noble Nook.

Producing this book was challenging for me because besides being the author, I was also the illustrator. With God's help I managed to get through it and I was actually pleased with the outcome!

Twirly Shirley and The Tsunami Mommy

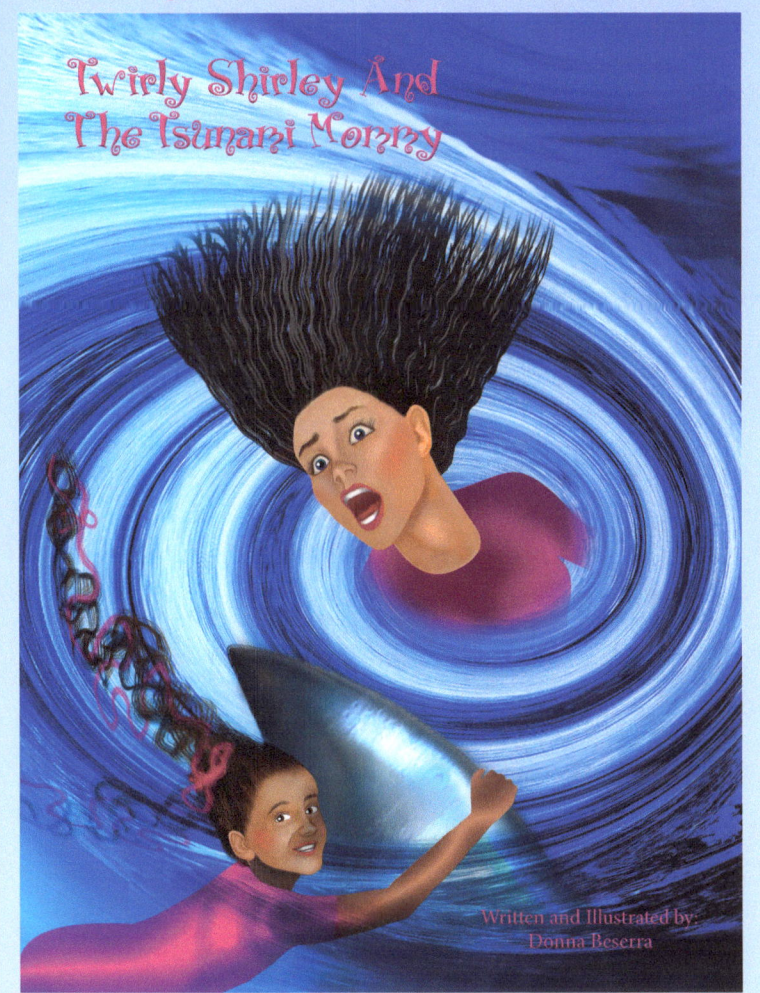

Great gift! Perfect for Mom's and kids alike. If you've ever been a mother, or had a mother, Twirly Shirley and the Tsunami Mommy is the book for you. Twirly Shirley, the girl with the wacky spinning braids is back for a brand new adventure, and this time she's brought along her very own Tsunami Mommy. Help your kids learn to deal their emotions in a fun and unique way.

Buffy the Butterfly's Apple Orchard

Buffy the Butterfly challenges kids to "Just put down that candy bar. Grab an apple and be a star!" This adorable little creature not only promotes healthy eating, she inspires kids to discover their talents by inviting them to join in the story.

"Buffy The Butterfly's Apple Orchard" is the first in the Creative Creatures Series. When I first began Creative Creatures, I had no idea where it would take me. As I was writing the books, I discovered a pattern. Each story featured a different child, creature and talent. Yet each book emphasized the same basic concept, that we are all unique, with our own special set of talents. Creative Creatures inspire children to discover those talents! So get those little brains A'tickin' with new ideas that keep on clickin'!

Creative Creatures help parents and teachers achieve their goals to educate by helping children to create. Now kids look deep inside themselves and leave their gadgets on the shelves. Creative Creatures make learning fun, and this adventure's just begun. There are more creatures on the way. Creative Creatures are here to stay. So get those little brains a'tickin with new ideas that keep on clickin!

Barton the Bat's Pumpkin Patch

Join Barton, the creative little bat, as he entertains in his exciting pumpkin patch adventure. You've never met a bat like Barton, and he'll inspire children to be just as unique and inventive as he is.

Barton emphasizes individuality by encouraging kids to be resourceful, notice the world around them and use their own ideas to develop their creative potentials. "Whatever it is, let it be you. Your personality should shine through." Barton stirs the imaginations of children in a special way.

I kept expecting to see royalties, but I continued seeing zeros, both with Createspace and Ingram Spark. Then one day I received a bill for over $200. Some of the books Barnes & Noble had ordered were returned because they hadn't sold, so I had to pay Ingram back. I was frustrated, but I knew the story wasn't over yet. I kept praying and believing.

I attempted to set up a Book Launch Party for *Twirly Shirley and the Tsunami Mommy*. I had planned to promote the book for Mother's Day which had already passed. The Book Launch was delayed until the end of July. I did the best I could with that date, but it was a let down when not one person showed up. I knew everything was okay though, and God was still in control.

Even though I did not see any sales, I knew interest in my books was growing. I had created pages for each title on Facebook. I was getting more and more viewings and likes as time went by.

I also knew children loved the stories I had written. I'd seen it many times during my school visits. The smiles on their faces told me a lot. I'd even met several kids who had read my books already. It surprised me sometimes, because I had not seen royalties. Yet somehow the kids knew about my books and enjoyed the stories.

My next title was *Maurice the Mouse's Cornfield*. I had already been working on it while I was planning the launch of the Tsunami Mommy. I worked diligently on the illustrations. I did struggle somewhat, especially with the cornfield. Fortunately I got great advice from my good friend, Melody Karns Trone. Before long I had created a finished illustration of my first cornfield. I completed the rest of my pictures and worked on the book layout.

After finishing the main story content, I had one more component. I needed to create Maurice the Mouse's Candy Cornfield Cake so I could include a recipe in the back of the book. I had designed the cake before, but this time it would be more difficult because I didn't have enough gummy mice. I would have to make my own candy creatures. I decided to shape the mice out of homemade fondant. It worked really well. I even added a candy corn on the cob.

I inserted an illustration of Maurice the Mouse holding the cake in the back of the book. Then I added the recipe. I thought it was a wonderful way to conclude the story! Now the book had been published and I was ready to start promoting it.

I had advertised *Maurice the Mouse's Cornfield* Online. My next step was to write a news release to submit to the media, and to set up a book launch party for Maurice. You see, publishing the book is actually just the beginning. There is a lot more work to be done after publishing. Advertising and marketing can take a lot of effort.

Maurice the Mouse's Cornfield

Maurice the Mouse's Cornfield is a tall tale told by a small creature. It is a great Midwestern Adventure that describes corn detasseling from a mouse's point of view. Maurice inspires young writers and speakers in his own "corny" way. Full of twists, turns and adventure this story is a great read!

There is so much more information I could include about my book publishing experiences, but I will save some of it for later. I don't think this will be my only autobiography. In fact, I already have new ideas for another one in the future. This story has just begun!

I would like to share just a little more about my experiences because it may help others who are facing similar circumstances. In addition to all the other struggles I've been through, I have actually endured physical pain and exhaustion from working long hours producing books. I've suffered eyestrain from staring at computers, and pain in my back from being hunched over a laptop.

For a long period of time I struggled with extreme pain and numbness from my neck to my fingertips. It was the type of pain one gets from slamming a door on his or her fingers. I'm not sure if this was caused by my publishing work or not. I do know that the situation was aggravated by the long hours I spent producing books.

During the time of my illness I read a book by fellow author which was very helpful and encouraging to me. My pastor at MGT New Hope Church, (Pastor Scott Reece) had written a book called *Thirty-One Days Of Healing (Living in Divine Wholeness)*. I studied this book along with my daily bible reading. The good news is that I am in much better shape now, because God has healed me and strengthened my hands. I am now well equipped to create books!

Dr. Rebecca Bravard of Quad City Spine Clinic also helped me during my recovery. I believe God works through doctors, and she was a definite blessing. Dr. Bravard not only helped by aligning my spine, she also suggested I set my laptop at a higher level to decrease the strain on my back. My daughter Sabrina later surprised me by allowing me use her large Wacom Tablet which also made my artwork much easier, an answer to prayer. It was set up closer to eye level and everything was enlarged.

Once this book is finished, I plan to get back to my animated version of *Twirly Shirley in My Sister the Twister*. I will also be creating a new version of *Pirate the Parrot's Tropical Treasure*. I expect to have these projects finished sometime in 2018.

Of course I have more books to write. I also hope to have animated versions of all my Twirly Shirley stories. I think it would be wonderful for the Creative Creatures Series to be performed on stage. These are things I envision for the future, and I thank God for the opportunities he has given me.

Although I may not have money coming out of my ears (yet), my books are serving their purpose even if it is on a small scale. Every child matters. Each child that has been blessed by my stories, has made my work well worth the effort. Yet I know in my heart that God will multiply the reach of my books. I don't know exactly how or when. I just know it will be soon.

Coming Soon!

Join Pirate the Parrot and Esther the Jester as they inspire and entertain in this tropical treasure of a tale!

www.ingramcontent.com/pod-product-compliance
Lightning Source LLC
Chambersburg PA
CBHW041125300426

44113CB00002B/66